PAUL SHEFTEL   PHYLLIS LEHRER

PERSONAL TRAINER
A Keyboard Musicianship Enrichment Program

including
TECHNIQUE
SIGHT-PLAYING
THEORY
REPERTOIRE

Volume 1

YBK Publishers, New York

PERSONAL TRAINER: A Keyboard Musicianship Enrichment Program

YBK Publishers, Inc.
39 Crosby St.
New York, NY 10013

http://www.ybkpublishers.com

ISBN: 978-1-936411-01-6
Library of Congress Control Number: 2011920429

Manufactured in the United States of America
(or in England when for sale outside of the United States)

rev ver 11-09

OVERVIEW

Personal Trainer is a program offering musical workouts and enrichment activities for piano students of many ages and skill levels. The overall structure consists of five books, each containing four sections dealing with specific issues. These four sections are entitled:

- Explorations

- Eye-So-Metrics

- Foundations

- Repertoire.

We believe the development of technique, sight playing and analytical skills are part of an integrated approach to total musicianship; all are stepping-stones to aesthetic expression and musical understanding. We want our students to feel comfortable as they learn to hear what they see, see what they hear, and grow in their understanding of the building blocks of music. Those, simply stated, are fundamental goals of *Personal Trainer.*

EXPLORATIONS
(Keyboard Skills)

We have wanted to avoid the notion of exercises as simply drills to be endured, hence the title "Explorations." This section does indeed consist of short examples grouped, for the most part, in clusters. In each cluster familiar keyboard patterns are explored that focus on varieties of physical gestures and articulations. For example:

- Various dynamics and articulations are explored within the framework of five-finger patterns.

- Intervals and triads, both harmonic and melodic, are explored in many and varied ways.

- Suggestions for additional activities, such as transposition and improvisation, are supplied throughout.

- Practice pointers and technique tips are included throughout.

We attempt to banish the word and concept of "exercise," or "drill." We substitute "exploration" to underline the importance we attach to learning as a creative and inspiring activity.

EYE-SO-METRICS
(Sight-playing)

- The examples in this section are based in large part on arrangements of folk songs from many and diverse cultures. They are related in level of difficulty and content to the activities in the other sections; they provide a rich and carefully sequenced source of materials for attaining fluency in this essential skill.

- Keeping a steady pulse is a vital part of sight-playing. We believe that sight-playing in an ensemble setting is an invaluable approach to achieving this goal. In each example we have provided a second part, at a similar level, as an option suitable for a teacher, fellow student, parent, sibling or friend.

FOUNDATIONS
(Keyboard Theory)

In the Explorations section we offer many activities intended to help students learn how to play scales and chords efficiently and fluently. There is a further fundamental issue: students, apart from learning the techniques of playing these basic structures, need to learn the underlying theory, particularly as applied to the keyboard.

- In Foundations we have included specifically designed activities to help students grasp these structures:

  - Scales are grouped according to fingerings.

  - Intervals and chords are grouped according to color schemes (keyboard geography).

- This material is presented in a logical, sequential and orderly fashion and supports most keyboard methods and curricula.

REPERTOIRE

As the title suggests, this section consists of examples of repertoire specifically chosen to support the activities and enrich the skills introduced in the preceding sections.

The repertoire has also been chosen for its intrinsic musicality and beauty. It is our hope that this repertoire will appeal to a large variety of tastes and ages and provide additional inspiration and enrichment to the program.

OTHER ISSUES

COORDINATING WITH METHODS

Every keyboard method differs in significant ways including presentation, development and sequencing of material. But there is considerable agreement on what needs to be covered and the importance of careful sequencing. Personal Trainer respects these considerations and is so designed as to fit into and support the structures of most methods.

DOSAGE

- Students and teachers already have very full plates. How can additional material be incorporated into already extensive study programs?

- "Dosage" is a possible solution. An investment, for instance, of only five minutes on a given section, might be considererd minimal. However, done on a regular basis, it would provide many students with a workout sufficient to promote considerable growth and enrichment to their ongoing routine.

- Teachers (and parents) know very well that the "ongoing routine" of many students is, at best, catch-as-catch can. An additional goal of Personal Trainer, with its carefully sequenced and structured materials, is to bring to students a heightened awareness of the value of efficient and thoughtful practice.

MIDI FILES

Every activity of Personal Trainer (with the exception of some repertoire) has a carefully designed accompaniment in the form of a MIDI file. These accompaniments provide an invaluable enrichment to the entire program.

The MIDI files can be used interactively with a computer program called *Home Concert Xtreme* from Zenph Sound Innovations. *Home Concert Xtreme* displays the solo part in music notation and plays the accompaniment tracks in a musically coordinated fashion by following your tempo and dynamics. *Home Concert Xtreme* will even turn the pages for you!

For more information about obtaining the MIDI files please visit my website: www.paulsheftel.com

To purchase *Home Concert Xtreme* or to download a completely free demo version of the program, or to see a demonstration on video, please visit: www.zenph.com

Home Concert Xtreme is a remarkable tool, well worth your investigation!

EXPLORATIONS

In our general preface we note our preference for the word "explorations" in contrast to "exercises." The obvious difference is that practicing an exercise, so called, can be a repetitive, dreary, monotonous and often an unproductive experience; an exploration suggests an investigation, a creative undertaking, a way of deriving maximum intellectual, physical and musical benefit from an activity.

- "Explorations" are presented with different options for investigation:

    - Varied approaches to finger, hand and arm movements.

    - Transpositions

    - Improvisations

    - Practice pointers and technique tips

- MIDI accompaniments add colorful musical dimensions, challenges and motivation. They can also serve as an effective musical metronome. Students may profit from using these accompaniments as they might a metronome, for the purpose of gradually increasing speed.

- The "explorations" are grouped in clusters so that considerable reinforcement is provided and students can view the same issue from different vantage points.

- This level contains 29 examples. A simple calculation would suggest that maintaining an average of only two a week would require a minimal investment of a student's (and teacher's) time. This scheme would allow a student to complete a level in the equivalent of one semester of work.

PURPOSE OF THE EXPLORATIONS

Listen: For rhythm, intervals, shapes, patterns, articulation.

Feel: Comfort within five-finger patterns and beyond. Be aware of fingering, coordination and ease in body, arms, wrist.

See: On the page and on the keyboard what is heard, felt, and understood.

Understand: How to transpose and how to improvise within and beyond the exercise patterns.

Have Fun: Listening to and playing with the accompaniments which support and enhance the exercises.

FINDING 5^{THS}

PRACTICE POINTERS

- Notice how the interval of the 5th is explored: whether playing legato, articulated or staccato, stay close to the keys and use circular and rotary forearm motion.

- Practice moving from one position to the next by "blocking" the 5ths.

- Always play on the upper left corner of the thumb tip so as to feel a strong connection to the key and free the wrist.

- Pull up on the pinky tip so you can feel the key and have control of the sound you want to produce.

- Feel the pulse of the meter before playing.

TECHNIQUE TIPS

- Always check your posture Sit tall. Feet planted firmly support a strong body. Feel that there is space and freedom in arms, elbows, and wrists; feel free and buoyant. Gently curve fingers.

- Your distance from the piano keyboard should allow you to reach the keyboard easily.

- Your feet ground your body. (Small children should use a special pedal box, or sit back on the bench and cross their feet at the ankles.)

- Adjust the music rack so that you can see the music easily.

ACTIVITIES

1. Find 5ths everywhere. (The two keys are always the same color except for the combinations B – F# and B♭ – F),
2. Play exercises with different articulations (staccato, legato and slurred notes.)
3. Shift articulations.
4. Make up new exercises using 5ths. Play these using different MIDI accompaniments included in this cluster .

DOWN UPS

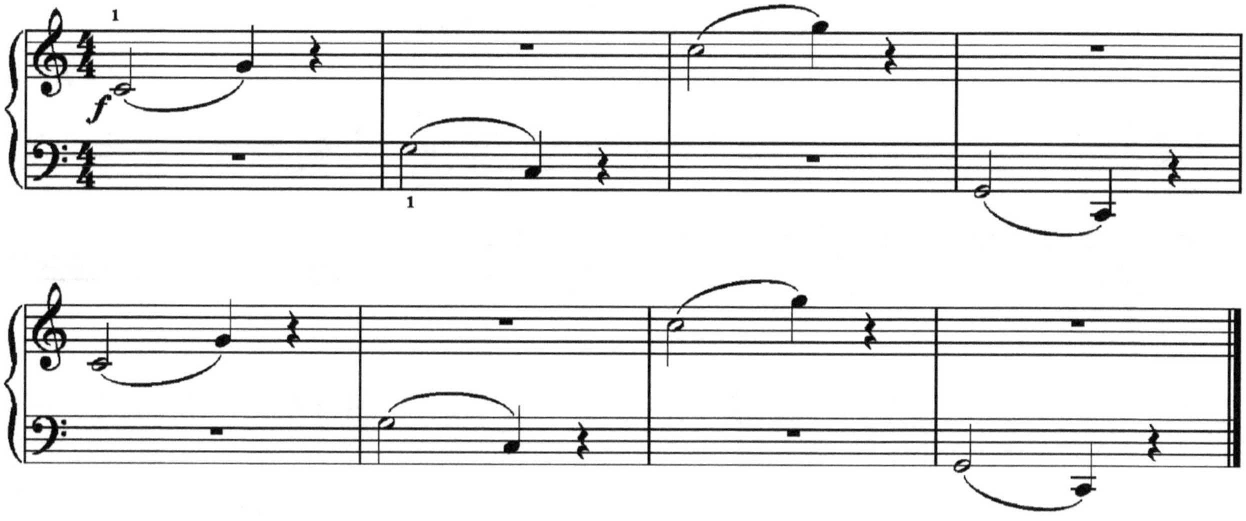

CHUG ALONG

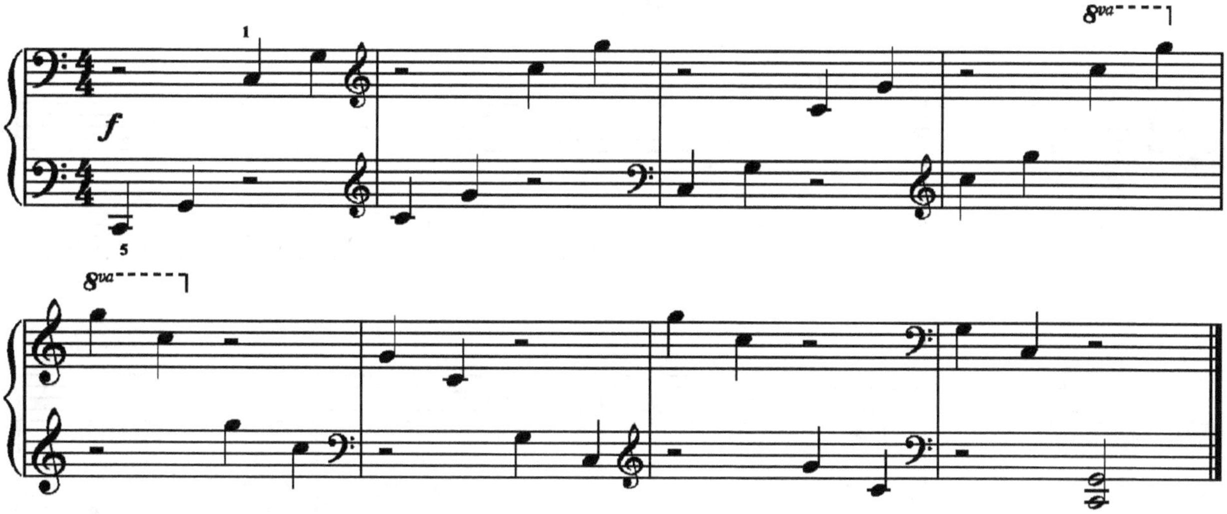

MOVING AROUND

ROTATIONS

INTERVAL EXPLORATION

TECHNIQUE TIP

The size of the interval will affect the degree of forearm rotation. Release your wrist before each rest.

BALANCING ACT

ACTIVITIES

1. Transpose to black keys
2. Play hands together

TECHNIQUE TIP

Begin with a dropping motion; end with a gentle rolling up motion

PUSH UPS

ACTIVITIES

1. Shift articulations
2. Transpose to F and G

INS AND OUTS

ACTIVITIES

1. Play staccato
2. Transpose to G
3. Play hands together (contrary motion)
4. Improvise 5-finger patterns to the accompaniment

CONTRASTS

ACTIVITY

Transpose to D and A.

CLOSING IN

ACTIVITY

Improvise questions and answers, each two measures in length, to the accompaniment.

FINGER PLAY - RIGHT ON

FINGER PLAY - LEFT ALONE

ACTIVITIES

1 Transpose first to D and A, then to D♭ and A♭.
2 Try playing hands together using parallel or contrary motion.

FILLING IN 5^{THS}
(5 FINGER PATTERNS)

TECHNIQUE TIP

A combination of forearm rotation and circular motions are desirable in performing these examples.

UPS AND DOWNS

ACTIVITY

Transpose to F and F# major.

BOUNCING ALONG

TWISTS AND TURNS

TURN AND GLIDE

BOUNCE

ACTIVITIES

1. Transpose to E and E♭
2. Try playing in parallel motion with hands crossed.

CHROMATICS

TECHNIQUE TIP

When moving between black to white keys, be aware of slight adjustments necessary in the arm and wrist.

SLINKY

Slinky, Pop-Ups, and *Step-Ups* all use fragments of the chromatic, or half- step scale.

ACTIVITY

Try playing a chromatic scale up and down, from C to C, one octave apart.

> Fingering:
>
> • thumb on white keys
>
> • middle finger on black keys
>
> • fingers 1-2-3 in the gaps (B-C-D♭ : E-F-G♭)

POP-UPS

STEP-UPS

TRIAD STUDIES

PRACTICE POINTER

The triads in the following examples are mostly presented in "broken" form (one note at a time). Practice in "block" form first.

TECHNIQUE TIP

Play block chords with supple arms and hands to avoid harsh sounds and tension.

TRIADS I

TRIADS II

TRIADS III

ACTIVITY

In the "Foundations" section there is a "color scheme" (see page 45) for practicing major triads. Following the order of this chart, practice these examples in all keys.

In the case of Triads III figure out the relationships of the three different positions. (Were one to start on D, for instance, the relationship C, F, and G would become D, G, and A.)

A LITTLE SAD

TAKE-OVERS

SHINE OR RAIN

These examples all use the C minor triad or alternate between C major and C minor.

Major triads are transformed into minor by simply lowering the third a half step.

ACTIVITY

Transpose these three examples into as many different keys as you are able.

EXPANSIONS

TECHNIQUE TIP

As intervals expand, move arms and elbows out from the body to align with and guide the hands.

STRETCHES I

STRETCHES II

STRETCHES III

ACTIVITY

Examples II and III use all the notes of the C scale. Transpose to G and D major—
and other keys as well.

GRAND FINALE

TWISTER

ACTIVITIES

1. Transpose to B and B♭.

2. Twister consists of four phrases of four measures each.

   • Improvise four phrases in a similar manner. The MIDI accompaniment, without the solo, can be used.

   • Work first with one hand, then both, using parallel and/or contrary motion.

BOOK 1—EXERCISES	DATE
DOWN-UPS	
CHUG ALONG	
MOVING AROUND	
ROTATIONS	
BALANCING ACT	
PUSH-UPS	
INS AND OUTS	
CONTRASTS	
CLOSING IN	
FINGER PLAY-RIGHT ON	
FINGER PLAY-LEFT ALONE	
UPS AND DOWNS	
BOUNCING ALONG	
TWISTS AND TURNS	
TURN AND GLIDE	
BOUNCE	
SLINKY	
POP-UPS	
STEP-UPS	
TRIADS I	
TRIADS II	
TRIADS III	
A LITTLE SAD	
TAKE-OVERS	
SHINE OR RAIN	
STRETCHES I	
STRETCHES II	
STRETCHES III	
TWISTER	

EYE-SO-METRICS

SIGHT-PLAYING TIPS

Scan music for:

- Key signature

- Time signature

- Clefs

- Rhythm patterns

- Note Patterns

    - Steps

    - Skips

    - Repeated notes

    - Changes of direction

- Melodic range

- Phrase structure

Choose a comfortable tempo

Maintain a steady pulse—and keep going!!

CANONS

Slowly   #1

Soulfully   #2

The remaining examples can be played as solos or as duets.

WELSH FOLK SONG

I

II

FRENCH FOLK SONG #1

I

II

GERMAN FOLK SONG

FRENCH FOLK SONG #2

I

With precision
(R.H. 8va when played with II))

II

With precision

RUSSIAN FOLK SONG #1

RUSSIAN FOLK SONG #2

I

II

MELODIES IN COUNTERPOINT

Paul Sheftel

I

Robustly
(8va when played with II)

II

Robustly

FRENCH FOLK SONG #3

I

FRENCH FOLK SONG #3

II

CZECH FOLK SONG

I

CZECH FOLK SONG

II

HAND IT TO ME

I

Paul Sheftel

HAND IT TO ME

II

Paul Sheftel

BOOK 1—READING	DATE
CANON #1	
CANON #2	
WELSH I	
WELSH II	
FRENCH #1 I	
FRENCH #1 II	
GERMAN I	
GERMAN II	
FRENCH #2 I	
FRENCH #2 II	
RUSSIAN #1 I	
RUSSIAN #1 II	
RUSSIAN #2 I	
RUSSIAN #2 II	
MELODIES IN COUNTERPOINT #1 I	
MELODIES IN COUNTERPOINT #1 II	
MELODIES IN COUNTERPOINT #2 I	
MELODIES IN COUNTERPOINT #2 II	
FRENCH #3 I	
FRENCH #3 II	
CZECH I	
CZECH II	
HAND IT TO ME I	
HAND IT TO ME II	

FOUNDATIONS

The rationale to this section is presented in the overview. In order to obtain a quick grasp of the contents we have provided "Goals at a Glance."

Different players, for innumerable reasons, will progress at a different pace. As players work through the suggested levels they should consult the appropriate "Fitness Challenge" in order to practice following a specific scheme.

The "Fitness Challenges" provide a way of evaluating the degree to which players have achieved a grasp of the material. Each of these has an optional MIDI accompaniment that provides additional challenges (as well, we hope, as additional motivation). Before players have reached the ability to do the "Fitness Challenges" in all keys they can still use the MIDI accompaniments up to whatever point has been reached.

GOALS AT A GLANCE

1. Major pentascales: all keys

2. Triads:
   Major: all keys
   Minor: with white key roots

3. Intervals:
   Perfect 5ths
   Major 2nds and 3rds
   Minor 2nds and 3rds

4. Scales
   C, G D, A, and E major, one octave

FITNESS CHALLENGE #1
PENTASCALES

etc. through all keys.

Continue through all keys by color groups:

I.   One color
     C – G

II. One black/one white (in the middle)
     D – A   D♭– A♭

III. One black/one white (to the side)
     F   F#

IV. Two black/two white
     E   E♭

V. Three black/three white
     B   B♭

FITNESS CHALLENGE #2
MAJOR TRIADS

etc. through all keys

Continue through all keys following the major triad color scheme:

I.   C, F, G and G♭ (one color)

II. A, D, E   A♭, D♭ and E♭ (One black/one white)
(Our reason for favoring this order is because it is easy to remember by using the
mnemonic "lemon<u>ade</u>.")

III. B   B♭ (Two blacks/two whites)

It can be helpful to find black-key/white-key patterns when locating different intervals on the keyboard. Here are some suggestions:

Perfect 5ths
- Always white key to white except for B to F#
- Always black key to black except for B♭ to F

Major 2nds (whole steps)
- Always white key to white or black key to black except in the gaps:
    E to F#; E♭ to F
    B to C#; B♭ to C

Minor 2nds (half steps)
- Always white key to black or black key to white except in the gaps:
    E to F
    B to C

Major 3rds
- White key to white starting on C, F and G
- Black key to black starting on G♭
- All others are either white to black or black to white

Minor 3rds
- White key to black starting on C,F and G; all others white key to white
- Black key to white except in the gaps:
    E♭ to G♭
    B♭ to D♭

FITNESS CHALLENGE #3
INTERVALS

Note:

Use this scheme for playing minor 2nds as well as major and minor 3rds. This scheme can serve for all intervals.

FITNESS CHALLENGE #4
MAJOR SCALE - ONE OCTAVE

FINGERING:

      Right hand: 4th finger on 7th scale step

      Left hand: 4th finger on 2nd scale step (7th step descending)

The same fingering is used for the G, D, A and E major scales.

FITNESS CHALLENGE #5
RHYTHMS

Tap or clap

#1

#2

#3

There are MIDI accompaniments available for these examples.

REPERTOIRE
PUTTING IT
ALL TOGETHER

The examples in this section are provided to enrich the musical experience. The level is approximately the same. Different styles are represented.

Mirror Mirror On the Waltz	Sheftel
March	Sheftel
February	Sheftel
Boogaloo in C	Sheftel
Give Me–Slap Me–Clap Me Five	Lehrer
Aller Anfang ist Schwer	Turk
Lullaby	Beyer
Dialogues 1 and 2	Bartok

MIRROR MIRROR ON THE WALTZ

(From *Excursions and Diversions*)

Paul Sheftel

Kind of waltzy

MARCH

(From *Excursions and Diversions*)

Paul Sheftel

FEBRUARY

(From *Excursion and Diversons*)

Paul Sheftel

BOOGALOO IN C

GIVE ME-SLAP ME-CLAP ME FIVE

Phyllis Lehrer

COUNT TO 5!

ALLER ANFANG IST SCHWER

(ALL BEGINNINGS ARE DIFFICULT
From *Short and Very Easy Pieces*)

Daniel Gottlob Turk
(1750-1813)

LULLABY

Ferdinand Beyer
(1803-1863)

DIALOGUE #1

(From First Term at the Piano)

Moderato

Bela Bartok
(1881-1945)

DIALOGUE #2
From *First Term at the Piano*

Bela Bartok
1881-1945)

ABOUT THE AUTHORS

PAUL SHEFTEL is a nationally recognized leader in the area of keyboard studies; his numerous published materials are widely used throughout the country. In his role as educator, he has performed, lectured, and conducted workshops in virtually every state in the United States. He has been a pioneer in the creation and development of instructional materials utilizing MIDI technology.

As part of the two-piano team of Rollino and Sheftel he performed throughout Europe and the United States, both in recitals and with such orchestras as the Berlin Philharmonic, the Royal Concertgebouw of Amsterdam, the Royal Philharmonic of London and the Chicago Symphony, among many others. He has appeared in two-piano and solo recitals in many of New York's leading concert halls, including Carnegie Hall, Town Hall, Alice Tully Hall, Merkin Hall, and Hunter College.

Mr. Sheftel is a graduate of the Juilliard School. His piano studies included work with Lazare Levy (in Paris), Edward Steuermann (at Juilliard) and Guido Agosti (in Rome on a Fulbright grant). Theory and composition: Mario Castelnuovo Tedesco and Alexander Tansman. In addition to his private teaching studio in New York City, he has served on the faculties of the Manhattan School of Music and Hunter College, has been piano editor for Carl Fischer, and is currently on the faculty of The Juilliard School where he teaches piano pedagogy.

PHYLLIS ALPERT LEHRER is known internationally as a performer, teacher, clinician, author, and adjudicator. She enjoys an active career as a soloist, collaborative artist, and clinician in the United States and such other coutries as Belgium, Canada, the United Kingdom, El Salvador, Taiwan, Japan, Sweden, Russia, Tajikistan, Brazil, and the Republic of Georgia. A founding member of the International Society for the Study of Tension in Performance, she contributes regularly to the Music Teachers National Association, the National Conference on Keyboard Pedagogy, and the World Piano Pedagogy Conference.

Ms. Lehrer's many articles, interviews, and reviews on piano pedagogy, music, and health have been published nationally and throughout the world. Her CD's include solos and duos with pianist Ena Bronstein Barton. In March of 2007 she was honored as a Music Teachers National Association Foundation Fellow, a program that "honors deserving individuals who have made significant contributions to the music world and the music teaching profession."

Ms. Lehrer has a Bachelor of Arts degree from the University of Rochester with music studies at the Eastman School of Music and a Master of Science in Piano from the Juilliard School of Music. Her teachers have included Paula Hondius, Lily Dumont, Adoph Baller, and Adele Marcus She is currently professor of piano and director of graduate piano pedagogy at Westminster Choir College of Rider University in Princeton, N.J.